The illustrations in this book were first published in *My Own Book of Bible Stories* and *My Own Book of Prayers*, copyright © Lion Hudson IP Limited

Bible text by Lois Rock
Prayers written and compiled by Su Box and Deborah Lock

Published by
Lion Hudson Limited
Wilkinson House, Jordan Hill Business Park,
Banbury Road, Oxford OX2 8DR, England
www.lionhudson.com

ISBN 978 0 7459 7903 8 (Bible hardback)
ISBN 978 0 7459 7905 2 (Bible gift edition)
ISBN 978 0 7459 7904 5 (bind-up edition)

First Bible hardback edition 2005
First Bible gift edition 2008
First Prayers hardback edition 2011
Second Bible hardback edition 2021
Second Bible gift edition 2021
This first bind-up edition 2021

A catalogue record for this book is available from the British Library

Printed and bound in China, September 2020, LH54

My Very Own Bible and Prayers

Bible retold by Lois Rock
Prayers written and compiled
by Su Box and Deborah Lock
Illustrated by Carolyn Cox

LION
CHILDREN'S

Contents

The Old Testament

The New Testament

My Very Own Prayers

My World

My Day

Our World

Sad Days

Happy Days

Introduction

Do you like exciting stories about people's lives? Stories that inspire you or make you pause and think? All the stories in this book come from the Bible. They were written a long time ago by many different writers over many years. The writers wanted to share the story of God's relationship with people. The Bible is a collection of books, which have been split into two sections. The Old Testament contains the stories and writings about God's people from the beginning to before the coming of Jesus. The New Testament covers the life and teachings of Jesus and his first followers, spreading his message about God. Even though these stories are about God and the people who lived a long time ago, their stories are still told as a guide for people today.

My Very Own Bible

The Old Testament

God Makes the World

In the very beginning, there was nothing – a huge dark nothing like a dark and stormy sea.

God spoke into the nothing: 'Let there be light.' At once, the light shone. God called the light 'Day' and the dark 'Night'. That was the first day.

Then God said, 'Let there be space around the world.' God called the space 'Sky'. That was the second day.

Then God said, 'Let the water come together so land will appear.' The water flowed into deep green pools and the brown land emerged. God called the water 'Sea' and the land 'Earth'.

God spoke again: 'Let the earth produce all kinds of plants.' Soon there were shy seedlings and bright flowers, nodding grasses and tall trees. God was pleased with all that had been made as the third day ended.

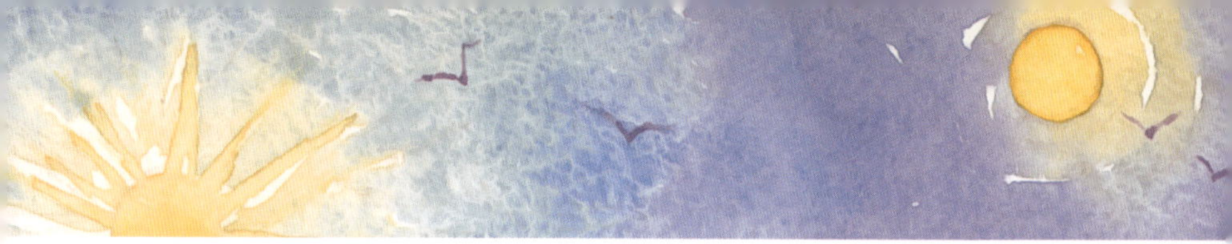

Then God said, 'Let there be lights in the sky: the sun for the day, and the moon and stars for the night.' The sun set on God's good world, and the fourth day ended.

Then God said, 'Let there be fish in the sea and birds in the air.' And so it was, and the fifth day ended with the sound of birdsong.

Then God said, 'Let the world be filled with animals.' There were animals of every kind: lumbering hippopotamuses and tiny shrews, graceful gazelles and yawning lions. God smiled. 'And now, let us make human beings to take care of everything that has been made.' God created man and woman and blessed them: 'May you have children, and may you feel at home in the

world. Everything in this world is for you to enjoy.' That was the sixth day.

In this way, the whole wide world was made. On the seventh day God rested, and God said that each seventh day was to be a time for rest and enjoyment for evermore.

The Garden of Eden

God planted a garden in Eden. It was a beautiful place, watered by a rippling river and shaded by green trees that bowed under the weight of their ripening fruit.

God put the first man, Adam, in the garden, to take care of it. Adam knew all the animals by name, but his only true friend and companion was the first woman, Eve.

In the middle of the garden stood a special tree. Its fruit gave knowledge: knowledge of what is good and what is bad.

'You must not eat from that tree,' warned God. 'If you do, you will die.'

Adam and Eve were perfectly happy in their paradise garden. Then, one day, a snake came slithering by.

'I've heard a whisper,' said the snake to the woman, 'that you're not allowed to eat from all the trees here.'

'Oh yes we are,' said Eve. 'Only one is forbidden; if we eat its fruit we will die.'

'Stuff and nonsense,' simpered the snake. 'It will make you wise. God must be afraid you'll get too wise. Try some.'

Eve wondered. The fruit did look lovely.
So she ate a little and gave some to Adam.

They looked at each other: suddenly they saw everything differently, and they knew they had made a terrible mistake. That evening, when God came into the garden, they hid.

God knew what had happened. 'You can no longer stay here,' said God. 'You must go out into the wide world where you will find good things and bad things all mixed together. Your life will be hard, and one day you will die.'

Adam and Eve had to say goodbye to paradise. All that was left was a dream of the time when the man and woman were close friends with God.

Noah and the Ark

Old man Noah sighed. 'Everywhere I go I see people doing the most wicked things,' he said. 'My three sons will have their own families soon; what kind of world will my grandchildren have to grow up in?'

Then God spoke to him: 'Noah, the world has become so bad that I am going to end it. I am going to send a flood; but you are a good man, and I am going to put you in charge of the new beginning.'

'Whatever shall I do?' asked Noah.

'Build a boat,' said God, 'the Ark. Make it big enough for you and your family and a pair of every

kind of animal. Take enough food to last a long time. I will keep you safe.'

Noah did as God said. As the rain began to fall, Noah led everyone safely onto his boat.

It rained for days and days. It rained so much that even the highest mountains disappeared. In all the world there was nothing left but Noah and his boat.

Then, one day, the Ark became stuck. 'We've hit land,' announced Noah.

Soon he could see mountain tops all around. He sent out a raven in search of land, and then a dove. The second time he let the dove fly, it brought back a fresh green leaf.

'Time to go and begin the world all over again,' cried Noah. The animals leaped and ran and scurried and scuttled into the world to make new homes for themselves.

‘The animals will have young,’ said God, ‘and you will have grandchildren.’

Noah and his family gave thanks to God for keeping them safe.

‘I am making you a promise,’ said God. ‘Never again will I flood the world. Look at the rainbow: it is a sign that, for as long as the world exists, there will always be summer and winter, springtime and harvest.’

Abraham and the Promise

'So I have become wealthy,' said Abraham to himself. 'That's what everyone in this town says. I have sheep and goats and camels and cattle, and they think that matters.'

Abraham sighed. He was wealthy. He had a beautiful wife, Sarah; but he had no son, and without a son everything else seemed worthless.

Then God spoke to him: 'I want you to go from here to a new land. It will be a land for your son, and for his children and their children, and for their children's children for ever. I will bless you, and your family will bring my blessing to all the world.'

Abraham was full of hope. He went with all his household to the land of Canaan. There they lived as nomads, always on the move in search of pasture and water for their flocks.

But the years went by, and still Abraham and Sarah had no son. Abraham sat outside in the cool of the night and wondered.

'Look at the sky,' said God. 'Your children's children will be as many as the stars in the sky.

'Look at the earth. Your children's children will be as many as the grains of sand.'

Still nothing happened. Then, one day, three mysterious travellers came by. As the men sat with Abraham eating a meal, they asked about his wife. 'Nine months from now she will have a son,' they said.

Sarah was listening nearby. 'Dear me!' she laughed. 'Don't those men know anything? An old woman like me can't have children. And Abraham's an old man!'

But the strangers' message was from God. Nine months later, Sarah had a son, Isaac. As the boy grew, Abraham learned more and more to have faith in God and in God's promises.

Joseph and the Wonderful Coat

Joseph was very proud of himself. He was wearing the wonderful new coat his father Jacob had given him. 'It's not just a coat,' he said to himself, 'more a promise that I'm the most important son in the family. Me! I'm the great grandson of Abraham, the grandson of Isaac, and the much-loved son of Jacob and his favourite wife, Rachel.'

Joseph had ten older brothers who were the sons of their father's other wife, Leah. They hated Joseph. The only brother Joseph got on with was his baby brother, Benjamin.

Joseph seemed to want to make everyone jealous. 'Listen to this,' he said. 'I had a dream. We were in the fields tying up sheaves of wheat. Then my sheaf stood up and your sheaves bowed down to it. What do you make of that?'

The brothers scowled.

Another time he said, 'I had another dream. The sun, the moon and eleven stars bowed down to me.' That even made his father angry. 'Don't dare to think that your whole family is going to worship you!'

But while the ten older brothers had to work hard looking after the sheep, Joseph stayed at home. One day, Jacob sent Joseph to see how the brothers were getting on.

'Here's our chance,' they said. 'Let's get rid of him.'

In a moment of anger they planned to kill Joseph.

'Wait! I've a cleverer idea,' said one. 'Let's sell him to those traders I can see over there. They must be going to Egypt. Joseph will fetch a good price as a slave.'

The brothers sold him. They kept the wonderful coat and deliberately stained it with blood. They let Jacob believe that Joseph had been killed by a wild animal.

Jacob wept. Far away in Egypt, Joseph knew that his proud boasting had come to nothing.

Joseph and the Great Famine

'I never dreamed I'd be a slave,' said Joseph to himself. 'But even when that happened I tried to serve my master well. Now his wife has told lies about me, and I'm stuck here in jail with the cockroaches.'

Life was hard. But Joseph had a special talent: he could explain the meaning of dreams. For that, the other prisoners came to like him.

One day, in the palace, the king of Egypt had a dream that no one else could explain. Someone at court knew about Joseph. He was brought from jail to the king.

'Here is my dream,' said the king. 'I saw seven fat cows grazing, and

then seven thin cows came and ate them. Then I saw seven plump ears of corn, but seven shrivelled ears of corn came and ate them.'

Joseph explained. 'This is what your dream means: there will be seven years of plenty, with good harvests; then there will be seven years of famine, with bad harvests. You must find someone to take charge and store grain from the seven good years to last the seven bad years.'

The king chose Joseph. He became the second most important person in all of Egypt.

After seven good years, there were bad harvests everywhere. Far away, Joseph's family were

hungry. They heard that there was food in Egypt, and Joseph's older brothers came to buy some.

Humble and trembling, they bowed down to the man in charge of the food stores. They didn't know that it was Joseph.

Joseph recognized them. His heart was breaking. He knew that he wanted to be friends with his family again, and especially with his younger brother, Benjamin.

In the end, Joseph said who he was.

'Let's forget the past,' said Joseph. 'God was taking care of us all the time. God sent me to Egypt ahead of you, so I could take care of you now.'

He invited all his family to come to Egypt. There, they were safe for many years.

The Baby in the Rushes

Little Miriam loved her new baby brother. But her mother had been crying and crying ever since he was born.

'It's not safe for a baby boy here in Egypt,' her mother explained. 'Our people came here hundreds of years ago, when there was no food in our own land. We were welcome then, but the man who is king now only wants us as slaves. He even wants all our baby boys to be thrown into the river.'

Miriam helped to hide the baby. As he grew bigger and noisier, the mother and daughter had to make a clever plan.

They took a basket and covered it with tar to make it waterproof, so it floated. Then they put the baby inside and hid him among the rushes at the edge of the river.

Miriam stayed close by to see what would happen. The princess of Egypt came down to the river to bathe. She saw the basket and she asked her servants to fetch it.

'Oh, a baby!' she cried. 'It must be one of the slave babies and someone's trying to save him. 'I want to rescue him too.'

Miriam stepped forward. 'Would you like someone to look after him for you?' she asked.

'Yes please,' said the princess. Miriam went to fetch her mother. The princess asked her to look after the baby until he was old enough to come and live as a prince in the palace.

'I shall call the baby "Moses",' said the princess. 'It is a name with a special meaning for me, to remind me of how I pulled him out of the water – and out of danger.'

The Great Escape

Moses grew up as an Egyptian prince, but he knew he was really one of the slave people.

One day, when he was grown up, he saw a slave being badly treated by a slave master. Moses was so angry he killed the slave master. That meant that he was in trouble, and he had to run for his life.

In the faraway wilderness he became a shepherd. One day, he saw a strange sight: a bush was covered with flames, but none of it was burning. He heard a voice speaking – it was the voice of God.

God told Moses to go and rescue his people. He must tell the king of Egypt to let them go free.

‘I won’t be any good at that,’ Moses argued. ‘I’m not good at talking.’

‘I will help you,’ said God, ‘and you can ask your brother, Aaron, to help you too.’

Moses did as God wanted. For a long time, the king said no. He did not want to let his slaves go free.

'God has told me that there will be disaster after disaster if you don't,' warned Moses. What Moses said came true. First the river turned blood red. Next came an invasion of frogs; then gnats, then flies. The animals died, and then the people fell ill. There were hailstorms; and great clouds of locusts flew in from the wilderness. Three long days were as dark as night.

The final disaster was the worst: the eldest son in every house in Egypt died. Amid the

sound of weeping, only the slave people were safe. God was taking special care of them.

At last the king said that Moses could take the people away. God led them through a marshy sea. When the king suddenly panicked and sent soldiers in chariots to fetch everyone back, the same marshes stopped them in their tracks.

'God has set us free,' cheered the people. It was a new beginning.

The Golden Box

Moses led his people out of Egypt. 'God will take us to the good land of Canaan, where we can make our home,' he told them.

The journey was long, and the wilderness was a dry and dusty place.

The people began to complain. 'We were better off in Egypt,' they moaned.

'God will take care of us,' promised Moses.

It was true. God helped Moses to find clean water for them to drink. God sent food called manna, which they gathered like flakes of frost, and plump birds called quails, which were easy to catch and good to eat.

Even so, the people were not happy. They were scared of going to Canaan, for other peoples already lived there.

Instead they spent years in the wilderness. In that time, Moses taught them how to live as God's people.

'You must love God more than anything,' said Moses, 'and you must treat other people as kindly as you want to be treated.

'You must worship God respectfully,' said Moses. 'As we travel, we have tents to live in. We must make a special tent for God, and it will remind us that God is with us.'

The tent was made of the finest materials and hung with curtains of blue and purple and red. The furnishings were made of gold. At the very heart was a golden box, and in the box was a copy of God's laws.

'The box is the sign of God's promise to us,' said Moses. 'God is our God, and we are God's people.'

The years went by. The people slowly began to understand how to obey God.

'I am old now,' said Moses, 'too old to go to the new land. Brave Joshua will lead you there, and you will find out that you really can trust in God.'

Joshua and the Battle of Jericho

'Look,' said Joshua to the people. 'Over there is the land where God has said we can make our home.'

It was a good land, but the people were worried. There were still other nations living there. How were they going to claim land for themselves?

Fortunately, their leader, Joshua, was a brave soldier, and he was also someone who kept God's laws.

'First we must cross the River Jordan,' he said. 'The priests will go first into the water, carrying the golden box that is the sign of God's promise. When they are standing in the water, God will make a way for all of us.'

By a miracle, the river dried to a trickle and everyone crossed safely into the land of Canaan. They came to the first city: Jericho, surrounded by high walls and defended by soldiers.

'God will help us take the city,' said Joshua. Every day for six days, the people marched round Jericho. Soldiers led the way; then came priests blowing trumpets, and more priests carrying the golden box. Behind them came the army.

The people inside Jericho grew more and more afraid. Was the army ever going to attack?

On the seventh day the same thing happened... only this time Joshua's people marched round a second time, then a third, and a fourth, and a fifth and a sixth and a seventh time.

'God has given you the city,' shouted Joshua to his soldiers. They gave a great shout, the priests blew their trumpets, and the walls fell down.

Joshua won the city of Jericho that day. Then he led the people further into the land. Sometimes they had to fight, but other times they made friends with the people they met in the new land and told them more about their God and the good laws they lived by.

When Joshua was old and the land was their home, he called everyone together. 'I and my family choose to live as God wants,' he declared. 'What will you do?'

'We promise to live as God wants,' the people all replied.

Samuel Hears a Voice

In a place called Shiloh, there was a special tent set aside for the worship of God. In the tent, the priests watched over a golden box: the special box that was a sign of God's promise to look after the people. Every year, people made a special journey to come and worship God there.

One year, Hannah came with her husband. She was very unhappy because she did not have any children. At Shiloh, she prayed to God, and she promised that if only she could have a son she would give him back to God, to serve God all his life.

By the next year, she had a baby, Samuel. When he was old enough, Hannah brought him to Shiloh to live there and help the priests.

Old Eli took care of Samuel. One night, Samuel was sleeping in God's tent when he heard a voice calling him.

He jumped up and ran to Eli. 'Here I am,' he said.

Eli was puzzled. 'I didn't call you,' he said. 'Go back to bed.'

A second time Samuel heard a voice and once again he ran to Eli.

'I didn't call,' said Eli. 'Go back to bed.'

The same thing happened a third time. Then Eli understood. 'Go back to bed,' he said. 'If you hear the voice again, say this: "Speak, Lord, for I am listening."'

God did speak to Samuel that night. The message was sad news for Eli: his sons were wicked, and God did not want them to serve him. Instead, God had chosen Samuel to be his servant.

God often spoke to Samuel, and Samuel grew wise. He became a great leader of his people and helped them to live as God's people should.

Samuel the Kingmaker

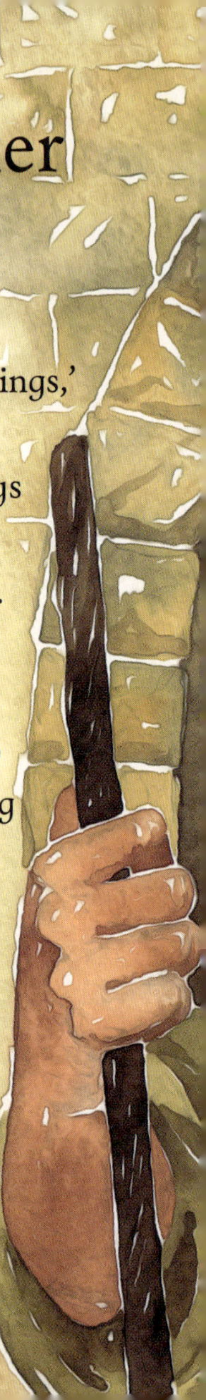

When Samuel grew old, the people came to tell him about their worries.

'The nations who live all around us have kings,' they said. 'We want a king to be our leader.'

Samuel shook his head sadly. 'Kings always end up treating their people like slaves,' he warned, but the people did not want to listen.

Samuel told God about the problem, and God told Samuel to let them have their way.

God also showed Samuel who to choose to be the people's first king – a handsome young man named Saul. At first Saul did well. He listened to Samuel's wise advice, he obeyed God and fought bravely.

Then he began to go his own way. He began to think he knew better than Samuel. God told Samuel that it was already time to choose the next king.

Samuel listened to what God said and then set off for the town of Bethlehem. There, he went to the house of a man named Jesse. 'I would like to see your sons,' Samuel said to Jesse.

One by one the young men came to meet Samuel. Samuel grew puzzled. None of them was God's choice. Had he made a mistake in coming here?

'Haven't you got any more sons?' asked Samuel, almost ready to give up.

'There's just one,' said Jesse, 'but he's only a boy. He's out looking after the sheep.'

Samuel asked to see him. Young David strode in, singing noisily and twanging a harp. 'This is the one,' Samuel thought.

He performed the ceremony of anointing with oil to show that David was God's chosen king.

‘You will not be king at once,’ said Samuel. ‘Not till after Saul.’

David smiled. He had grown up knowing about God and loving God, and now God had chosen him.

David and Goliath

King Saul frowned. The war against the Philistines was going badly. They were brave and cunning, and had strong iron weapons.

Saul's army were worried. They did not seem to be able to win. They had few weapons, and even those they had weren't very strong.

They all looked towards the Philistine army camped on the opposite hill.

As they watched, a giant man strode out. His helmet glittered in the sun and he carried a huge spear. Beside him was another soldier carrying a heavy shield with which to protect his master.

'I am Goliath,' roared the giant. 'Come and fight me. If you can find someone to beat me, then you will win, and we will go away. But if not...'

Saul's army shuddered with fear. Goliath's mocking laugh rang across the hills.

One day, David came to visit his brothers who were in Saul's army. Goliath came out and gave the challenge, as he did every day.

'How dare that Goliath think he can beat us!' said David. 'God is our helper.'

David's brothers thought he was simply being cheeky, but David really wanted to fight Goliath. When King Saul heard, he offered him his armour.

'It's too heavy,' said David. 'I know how to fight without that.'

He took his shepherd's stick and a sling that he used to hurl stones. Then he sauntered down towards Goliath, stopping to choose five pebbles.

'How dare you come to fight me like that?' roared Goliath.

'I dare because I trust in God,' replied David. At that, he took a stone and hurled it at the giant. Goliath fell.

Behind him, the army cheered. David had won! He was a hero!

Fearless King David

'David is our hero! He has beaten our enemies!' The people shouted and danced for joy.

King Saul should have been pleased, and in a way he was, but he was also very jealous.

'What if David tries to make himself king?' he worried. 'What will happen to me? What will happen to my son Jonathan?'

In fact, David and Jonathan had become best friends. When Saul, in a dark mood, made a plot to kill David, Jonathan helped him to escape.

David became an outlaw, living with a band of friends in the wilderness. Saul was desperate to find him and get rid of him, but God kept David safe.

All the time, the people's enemies, the Philistines, were watching. With David out of the army, they began to attack Saul and his men. In a great battle, Saul and Jonathan were both killed.

David wept for the friend he loved and the king he admired, but he knew that his time had come. He began to drive out his people's enemies. He captured a city on a hill and made it his own – the city of Jerusalem.

'This will be God's city,' he said. He arranged for the golden box that was the sign of God's promise to be brought into Jerusalem, and there was great rejoicing.

'I shall build a temple for God here,' thought David. When the people had lived in tents, it had

been right to have a tent for God. Now that they had homes and a homeland that was safe from enemies, they wanted a proper home for God.

'That is not for you to do,' God told him. King David's job had been to lead his people to victory and to peace.

Wise King Solomon

David's son Solomon became king after him. He was a young man, and the job of being king seemed very hard.

One night, in a dream, God asked him what he would want if he could have just one thing.

'I would want to be wise,' said Solomon. 'That is what I most need to rule your people well.'

Solomon did become wise. He became famous for the clever way he helped his people to settle their quarrels. He was famous for his wise sayings.

He also knew how to make good plans. He put himself in charge of building a temple for God – a temple of strong stone, carved cedarwood and the finest gold. The gold box that was a sign of God's promise was brought there, and priests led the people in worship.

In a land far away, the Queen of Sheba heard of Solomon's kingdom, of his wealth and his wisdom. She came with her servants and her camels and rich gifts. She came with the hardest questions she could think of, to test if Solomon was wise.

What she saw was even more marvellous than she had imagined. 'Truly,' she exclaimed, 'your God is good to you.'

For ever after, people remembered the time of Solomon as a time of gold.

Elijah and the Fire

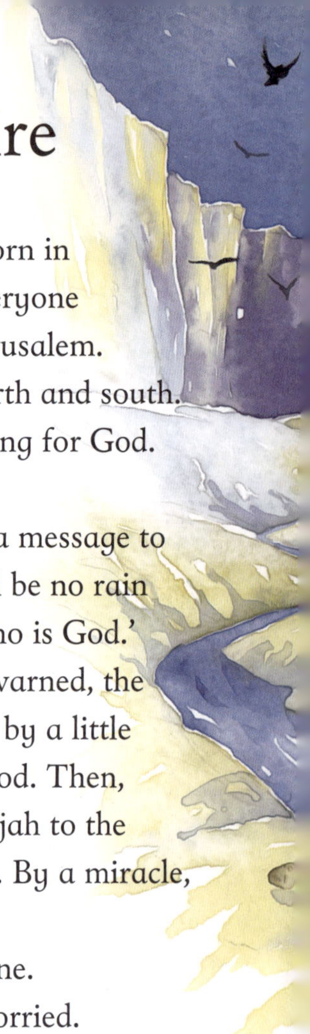

Elijah sighed. If only he had been born in the time of King Solomon, when everyone worshipped God in the temple in Jerusalem.

Now the people were divided, north and south. In the north, King Ahab cared nothing for God. He worshipped Baal.

Elijah was God's prophet. 'Take a message to Ahab,' said God. 'Tell him there will be no rain until I say so. Then he will know who is God.'

Elijah did so. Then, as God had warned, the land dried out. God kept Elijah safe by a little brook, where ravens brought him food. Then, even the brook dried up. God led Elijah to the home of a poor woman and her son. By a miracle, God provided enough food for the little household all through the famine.

In his palace, King Ahab grew worried. Was it ever going to rain again?

At last, Elijah came back.

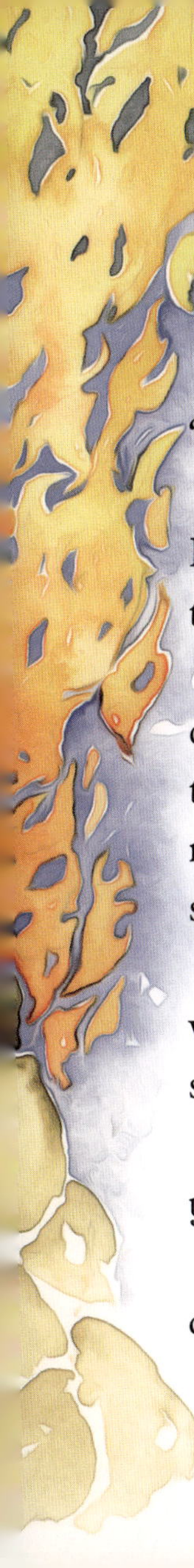

'Here comes trouble,' snarled Ahab.

'You are the cause of the trouble,' said Elijah. 'But now you are going to find out who is God.'

Elijah told the king to bring the prophets of Baal to a mountain for a contest in front of all the people.

First the prophets of Baal prepared an altar and laid their sacrifice on it. Then they called to Baal to set it alight. Nothing happened, and nothing happened. They called some more, and still nothing happened.

Then Elijah prepared his sacrifice. He poured water all over the altar till even the ground was soaked.

Then he said a prayer: 'Lord God, show that you are our God.'

The fire came blazing down onto Elijah's altar. 'The Lord is God,' everyone shouted.

That night, the rain came.

The Story of Jonah

Once upon a time there lived a man named Jonah. One day, God spoke to him: 'Jonah, I want you to go the city of Nineveh. The people there are very wicked. You must tell them to change their ways. If they don't, I will destroy them.'

Jonah did not want to go. He ran away and got on a boat that was going far, far away.

When the boat was at sea, a storm began to blow. The sailors were terrified.

'God must be punishing us,' cried the sailors. 'Someone here must have made God angry.'

Jonah had to tell the truth. 'I'm the one to blame,' he said. 'Throw me overboard or we'll all die.'

The sailors didn't want to harm Jonah, but the storm got worse. So they said a

prayer and threw him into the sea.

Jonah thought he was about to drown, but a big fish came and swallowed him. Inside the fish, Jonah had time to think. 'I'm sorry, God,' he said. 'I will always obey you from now on.'

The fish took Jonah to land and spat him onto a beach. Jonah hurried off to Nineveh.

'Change your wicked ways,' cried Jonah, 'or God will punish you.'

The people listened. The king listened. The king ordered everyone to say sorry to God.

Jonah was cross. 'The people of Nineveh deserved to be punished,' he muttered to God. 'You're too forgiving. It's not fair.'

Jonah sat and sulked. He sulked in the sun. He sulked in the shade. He sulked even more when the lovely plant that gave him shade died.

'Everything is so unfair!' he cried.

'Oh, you care about a plant, do you?' said God. 'Well, I care about the people of Nineveh and all their animals.'

The Fiery Furnace

God had given the people a land of their own. God had let them have kings to help protect them against their enemies. But as the years went by, the people and the kings often forgot about God. When they did, it seemed that everything went wrong.

Hundreds of years after the time of Solomon, the great enemy was the king of Babylon. His armies came and captured Jerusalem. Many of the people were taken away to Babylon itself.

One day, the king had a huge golden statue made of one of his gods and ordered everyone to come and see it. They all gathered. 'When my musicians play, everyone is to bow down to my statue,' he declared.

The music played. Everyone bowed down – everyone except Shadrach, Meshach and Abednego.

When the king heard about them, he was furious. 'If you will not worship the great god of Babylon, then you will be thrown into a fiery furnace,' he said.

'Our God can help us,' the three men replied. 'In any case, we won't worship your god.'

The king ordered the fire to be made seven times hotter than usual. Shadrach, Meshach and Abednego were bound hand and foot and flung into the flames.

The king looked to see his punishment working. He gasped: he could see four men walking in the flames, and one of them looked like an angel.

'Shadrach! Meshach! Abednego! Come out!' he ordered.

The men walked out. They were not burned; they were not singed. They didn't even smell of smoke.

'Their God sent an angel to rescue them,' said the king. 'Their God is a great God. I therefore order that no one is to say a word against the God of Shadrach, Meshach and Abednego.'

Daniel and the Lions

Daniel was loyal to God. Three times every day he went to the window that looked towards Jerusalem and said his prayers.

Daniel was also the best servant a king could have. Daniel had been a wise helper to the king of Babylon. When that king was beaten by the Persians, Daniel became the most important official in the court of King Darius of Persia.

The other officials were jealous of Daniel. They made a plan and went to see the king.

'O king, live for ever,' they said. 'We have agreed a new law. For thirty days, no one in your kingdom is to ask for anything from anyone, man or god, except yourself. Anyone who disobeys must be thrown to the lions.'

King Darius was pleased. It was a law to find out who was loyal and to get rid of anyone who wasn't. 'This is my law and it must not be broken,' he declared.

Then the men went to spy on Daniel. As soon as they saw him saying prayers to God, they rushed to tell the king.

'Your majesty,' they said. 'You made a new law that, for thirty days, anyone who asked for anything from any man or god except you should be thrown to the lions.'

'That is true,' replied the king. 'The law of Persia cannot be changed.'

Then the men said, 'Daniel does not respect you or your law. He prays to his God three times a day.'

Darius was most displeased. He did not want to get rid of his finest official, but his law was law.

Daniel was marched to the pit of lions. 'May your God help you,' whispered Darius. Then Daniel was thrown inside and the door was locked.

Darius worried all evening. When the next morning dawned, Darius rushed back to the lion pit.

'Are you still there?' he called to Daniel.

'O king, live for ever,' replied Daniel. 'God knows I have done nothing wrong, and God has kept me safe.'

Darius was overjoyed. Daniel was pulled to safety. 'Now throw Daniel's enemies to the lions,' Darius ordered. 'Everyone is to know that Daniel's God is the living God.'

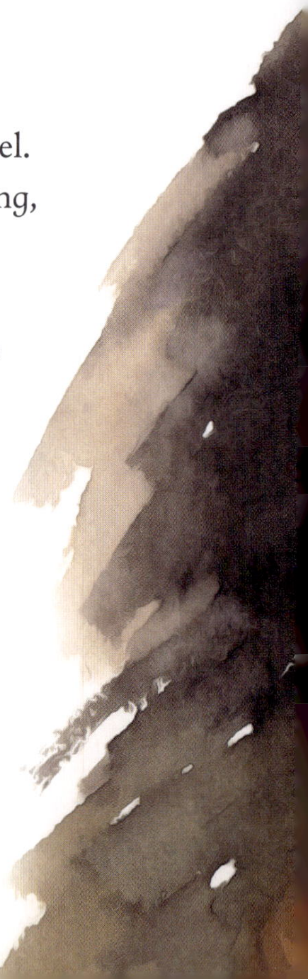

Nehemiah and the City of Jerusalem

God had promised to give the people a land of their own. When the people had forgotten about God, enemies had taken them far away, and Jerusalem had been destroyed. But God had promised to bring them home again.

The king who ruled them, King Cyrus of Persia, made a proclamation: 'Let God's people return to Jerusalem. Let them rebuild their temple.'

The people were overjoyed, and many went home. To their dismay, they found a ruin, and they wept.

But they were keen to work, and slowly they managed to build a new temple – not as grand as King Solomon's, but a temple all the same.

Back in Persia, Nehemiah still worked for the king. He was eager to hear how his people were getting on with rebuilding Jerusalem. He heard

that the city itself was still tumbledown. It didn't even have walls. Nehemiah wanted to help.

The king gave him permission to go, and Nehemiah made the journey. He rode his donkey around the city to see what needed to be done.

Then he came up with a plan. Every family was asked to build a length of wall. The plan was a great success.

The foreigners who lived nearby were angry and jealous. They tried to stop the building. Nehemiah arranged for half the people to build while the other half kept watch.

After fifty-two days, the work was complete. Jerusalem was a city with walls.

There was a great celebration. Everyone marched around the city. They sang and played music. Then they gave thanks to God – their God.

The New Testament

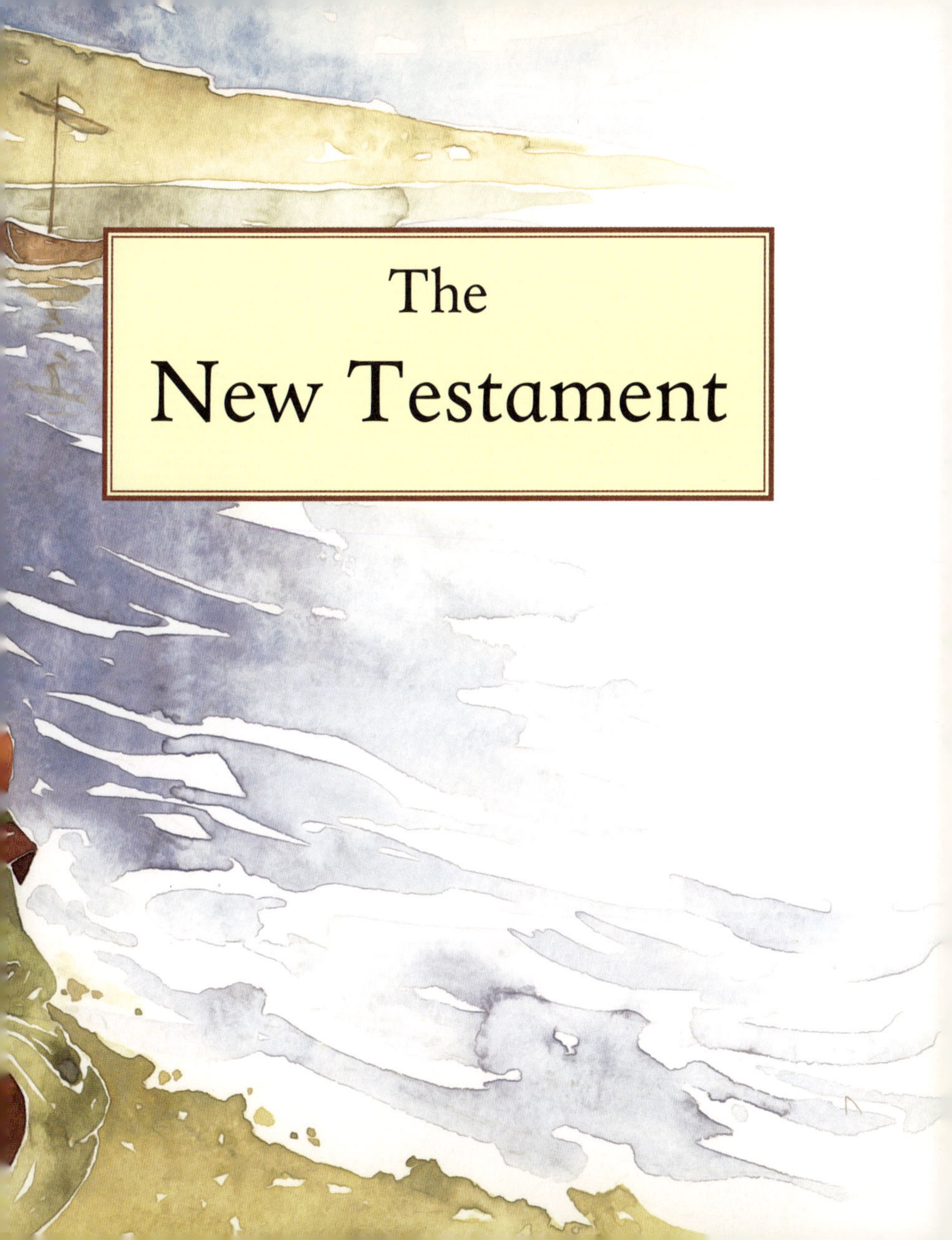

The Baby in the Manger

Mary lived in the little town of Nazareth. It nestled among the hills of Galilee, but the land was all part of the great Roman empire. Not that it mattered much to Mary – she was simply looking forward to getting married to a man named Joseph.

On one particular day, everything began as usual; but everything changed when an angel appeared.

'Mary,' said the angel, 'God has chosen you to be the mother of a baby – God's own son.'

Mary was puzzled. The message was hard to believe, and she didn't really understand it. But she loved God, and she replied, 'I will do as God wants.'

In a dream, an angel told Joseph to take care of Mary and her baby. Months later, when the baby was almost due, Mary and Joseph had to go on a journey together. The Roman emperor wanted to know how many people lived in his empire, so he could make them pay taxes. Everyone had to go to their home town, and so Mary and Joseph went to Bethlehem.

The town was very crowded. The only place where Mary and Joseph could shelter was in a stable for animals.

There, Mary's baby was born. She wrapped him warmly and laid him to sleep in the manger.

Out on the hills nearby, shepherds were looking after their sheep. Suddenly, the sky grew bright. An angel appeared. 'Here is good news for all the world,' said the angel. 'God's special king has

been born in Bethlehem. He is the Saviour, the Christ. You will find him snugly wrapped and lying in a manger.'

Then a thousand angels began to sing: 'Glory to God in the highest, and peace on earth.'

The shepherds hurried to Bethlehem. They found the baby, just as the angel had said.

The Wise Men and the Star

Away in the East, there lived some men who studied the stars. One night, they saw a bright new star. They knew at once what it meant.

'It is a sign that a new king has been born,' they said. 'We must go and find him.'

They made ready for a long journey and went on their way, always keeping the star ahead of them.

In time, they came to the city of Jerusalem. It was part of the Roman empire now, but scheming King Herod ruled over day-to-day matters. He had made the city beautiful, with a splendid new temple, but he had little respect for God. He cared only about being king.

He was angry when he heard that travellers had come in search of a new king. He called his advisers.

'Our people are hoping that God will send them a king, a Christ,' he said. 'Do we know where the king will be born?'

'In Bethlehem,' the advisers replied.

King Herod sent for the wise men and told them to go and look in Bethlehem. 'When you have found the king, come and tell me, so I can go and see him too,' he said. He smiled to himself. His wicked plan was to find the baby and kill him.

The wise men followed the star to Bethlehem. There they found Mary and Joseph and the baby Jesus. They offered him rich gifts: gold and frankincense and myrrh.

An angel warned the wise men not to go back to King Herod, but to go home another way.

In a dream, an angel told Joseph to escape with Mary and the baby to Egypt. There they were safe from the wicked king. Only when they heard he was dead did they return to Nazareth.

Jesus Grows Up

In the little school in Nazareth, Jesus listened carefully. He wanted to know all about the laws of his people, to learn what was right and what was wrong. He wanted to understand why his people believed that God was going to send a king to lead them to freedom. What sort of king did his teacher think that might be?

The more Jesus learned about God, the more he wanted to go to the temple in Jerusalem. Every year, at the time of a festival called Passover, a group of pilgrims went from Nazareth to the city, and Mary and Joseph went with them.

When Jesus was twelve, he was allowed to go. He saw the beautiful temple on the hill, gleaming in the sunshine. He saw the ceremonies that celebrated the time, long ago, when God had chosen Moses to lead his people to freedom. He saw the hundreds and hundreds of pilgrims, rich and poor, who had come to worship God from everywhere.

When the festival was over, the people from Nazareth set off for home. At twelve, Jesus was quite grown up, so the group had walked a long way before Mary wondered where Jesus was. Who had he been travelling with that day?

No one had seen him. 'This is terrible,' wept Mary. She and Joseph hurried back to Jerusalem.

The next two days they hunted high and low. On the third day they began to fear the worst.

Then, at last, they found Jesus: he was in the temple courtyard, sitting with the teachers, listening to them and asking questions.

'Where have you been? Why have you done this to us?' Mary cried.

Jesus was surprised. 'Surely you knew I had to be in my Father's house!' he replied.

Mary and Joseph did not understand; but Jesus went home with them and was a good and obedient son.

Jesus' New Beginning

Jesus had a cousin named John. When they were both grown up, John became much talked about. He lived out in the wilderness, preaching to anyone who came to listen. 'It's time to get ready to welcome God's chosen king,' he said. 'Give up your bad old ways and make a new start. God will forgive you.'

He baptized those who wanted to change in the River Jordan.

One day, Jesus came along. He asked to be baptized too. 'But you don't need to make a change,' said John. 'You're better than me.'

Jesus insisted. As John lifted him out of the water, he heard God's voice saying, 'This is my Son.'

After that, Jesus went off by himself in the desert. He wanted to be alone with God, to think about all that lay ahead. After forty days without food, Jesus heard the whisper of temptation: 'You're God's son. You could turn these stones into bread.'

Jesus had studied the writings of his people: the stories, the laws, the sayings of the prophets. 'No,' he replied. 'The writings say that we need more than bread in order to live.'

The whisperer spoke again: 'You could throw yourself down from the top of the temple. The writings say that God's angels would save you.'

'No,' replied Jesus, 'the writings also say that it

is not right to put God to the test.'

A third time the whisperer spoke: 'You could be king of the whole world. Serve me, and I'll help you...'

'Go away, Evil One,' replied Jesus. 'The writings tell us to serve God alone.'

Then the whisperer went away, and Jesus knew for sure what he must do.

Jesus and the Disciples

Everyone was talking about Jesus. 'Have you heard about the new teacher – the son of Mary from Nazareth? He's going round all the villages talking about God to anyone who will listen.'

'He says that God is welcoming everyone to be part of God's new kingdom, and that everyone must get ready.'

'He's working miracles too. That must mean he's special. He can heal people with just a touch, just a word.'

Jesus made his home in a little town on the shore of Lake Galilee. Among his friends were some of the men who fished the lake from little boats. One day, as he stood on the beach talking to the crowds who had gathered, he saw two boats moored in the shallow water. Jesus got into Peter's boat and asked him to push it further into the lake, so he could speak to the people from there.

Peter went back to washing his nets, but he found himself listening to what Jesus said.

When Jesus had finished talking to the people,

he asked the fishermen to go out a bit further and let their nets down for a catch.

Peter shook his head. 'It's the wrong time of day,' he said. Then he shrugged and did as Jesus had asked.

The nets filled with fish – so many that the nets almost broke as the men hauled them in.

'Leave your fishing,' said Jesus, 'and come and follow me.'

Peter and his brother Andrew, along with two other fishermen, James and John, became Jesus' close friends. Jesus called all kinds of people to follow him – rich

and poor, young and old, men and women. From them he chose twelve to learn from him and be his disciples: the four fishermen, then Matthew the tax collector and Simon, Philip, Bartholomew, Thomas, James, Thaddaeus and Judas.

Jesus the Teacher

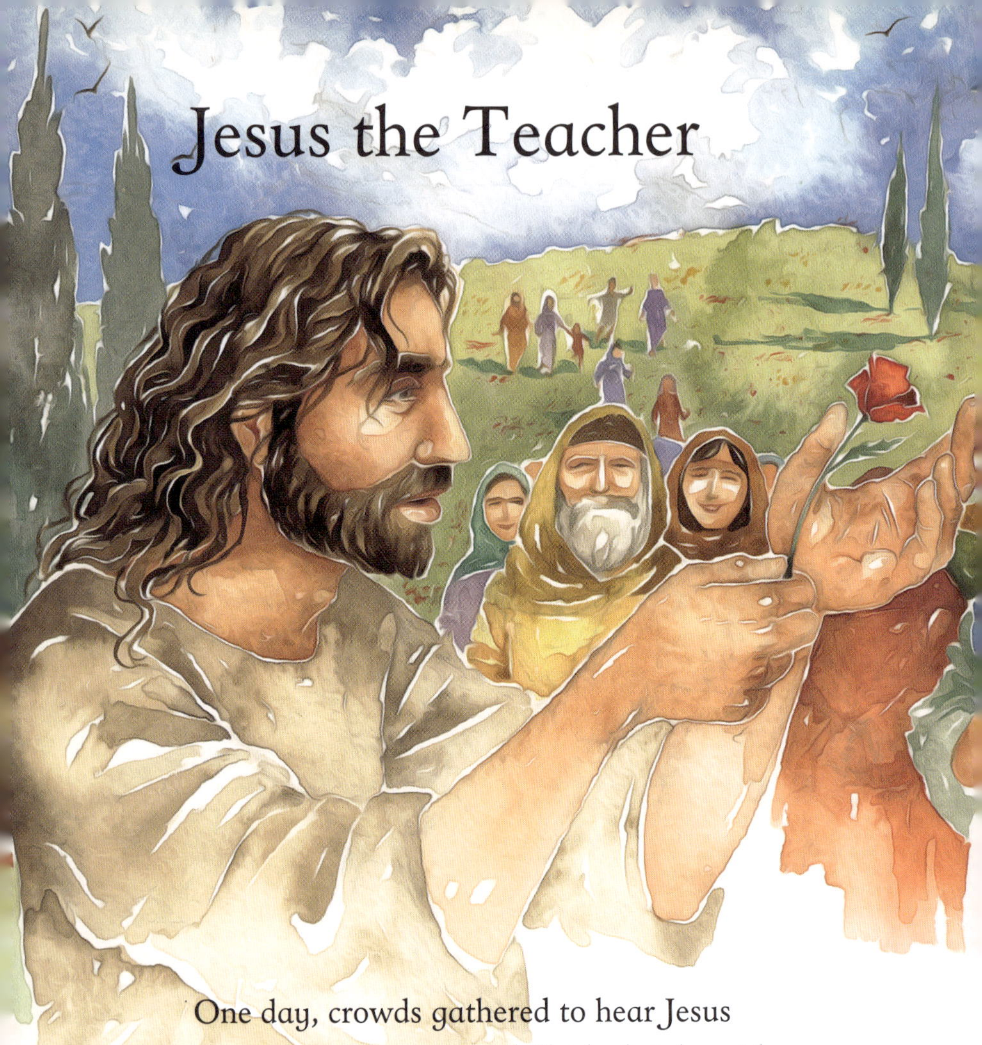

One day, crowds gathered to hear Jesus speak. They were on a hillside, bright with flowers, overlooking Lake Galilee.

'Think of all the things you worry about,' said Jesus. 'How will you make a living? Will you ever be rich? Will you always have enough to eat? Will you be able to afford the clothes you need?'

He picked a wild flower. 'Look at the flowers,' he said. 'They don't worry about what to wear. Yet the finery God gives them is more wonderful than even rich King Solomon ever wore.'

He waved towards the birds that fluttered among the bushes. 'Look at the birds. They don't worry about sowing and harvesting and gathering food for the winter. God provides all they need.

'And this is what I want to tell you: make it your aim to live as God wants, to do the things that really matter, the things that will

seem important in heaven. Remember to show love and respect to everyone, even those who hate you. If people treat you badly, forgive them, just like you would want to be forgiven. Do all these things and know that God will take care of you.

'Don't make a big show of doing good things. You may impress other people, but you won't impress God. When you give to someone who is in need, do it quietly, so only you and the person know about it. God will reward you.

'Remember to pray to God,' Jesus said. 'Don't show off about it, as some do. Go into a room alone, or to a quiet place.

'Here is a prayer to use:

“Our Father in heaven:
May everyone respect your holy name;
may your kingdom come.
May your will be done, on earth as it is in
heaven.
Give us today the food we need.
Forgive us the wrongs we have done,
as we forgive those who have wronged us.
Do not let hard times come upon us,
and keep us safe from the Evil One.”’

Jesus’ followers listened carefully. They wanted to remember all that he said.

Jesus and the Storm

Jesus was tired. He had spent the whole day talking to the crowds and helping those in need. As the sun began to set, he said to his friends, 'Let's take the boat over to the other side of the lake.'

The last of the sunlight sparkled on the water. As the shadows grew darker, Jesus fell asleep in the bottom of the boat.

The boat sailed peacefully across the lake. When it was about halfway, a chilly wind blew down from the hills. The boat began to rock, and the fishermen looked at each other, their faces showing their worry.

'Head for shore, and quickly,' they said, but it was too late. Already the wind was blowing more fiercely, and the waves were tossing the little boat up and down, up and down.

'This is bad, very bad,' muttered Peter. The water was crashing over the side of the boat now, and he was desperately trying to bale it out.

Then the boat dived into the trough of a wave and water poured in.

'Do something! We're going to drown,' shouted someone.

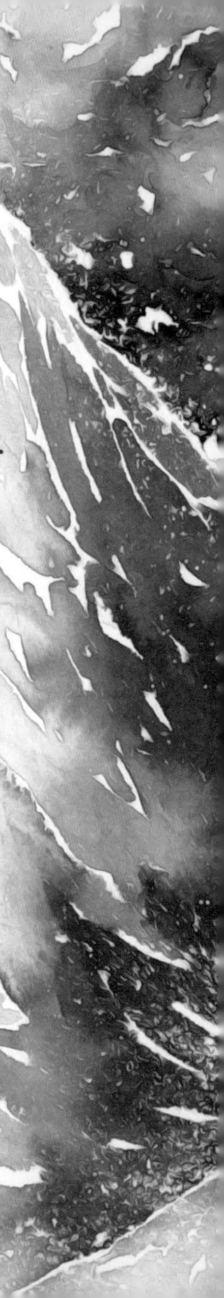

Another of the friends shook Jesus awake. 'How can you sleep! Don't you care what's happening!'

Jesus looked around. He saw the waves.

He saw his terrified friends. Then he stood up.

'Be quiet!' he said to the wind.

To the waves he said, 'Lie down now!'

At once the storm was over. The sea was calm, and the air was still.

'Why were you afraid?' asked Jesus. 'Why didn't you trust?'

The friends were really afraid now. Who was this Jesus, who could make the wind and waves do as he told them?

Jesus and the Hungry Crowd

Jesus and his friends were hoping for a restful day. They had taken the boat across the lake to a quiet place on the other side.

'I know where they're going,' someone said. 'We can walk there if we hurry.'

Even as Jesus and his friends arrived they could see hundreds of people rushing to the same place. 'I can't turn them away,' said Jesus. 'I must spend time talking to them.'

And so he did – all through the day, till the shadows grew long.

'You must stop now,' Jesus' friends said to him. 'Send the people to the towns and villages nearby where they can get something to eat.'

'We can't do that,' said Jesus. 'We must give them something.'

His friends were puzzled. 'We haven't got the money to feed a crowd,' they said. 'And where would we get food?'

'See who does have food,' said Jesus.

They asked the crowd, and a boy came forward with a small basket. Inside were five loaves and two small fishes.

'Ask everyone to sit down,' said Jesus. Then he took the food, said a prayer of thanks and began to give pieces out to his friends to share with the crowd.

To their amazement, there was enough for everyone. When the meal was over, the disciples gathered twelve baskets of scraps.

The following day, the crowd came back. 'Don't be hungry for the kind of bread you had yesterday,' he said. 'Be hungry for me and my teaching; then you will be satisfied for ever.'

Jesus Heals a Little Girl

The lake shore was as crowded as could be. Everyone was trying to catch a glimpse of Jesus, to get close enough to hear his teaching better.

Jairus came hurrying down. 'Excuse me,' he pleaded, 'can I get through?'

People grudgingly made way for him. After all, they'd got there first; but Jairus was one of the community leaders, and that made him quite important.

Jairus was almost in tears when he reached Jesus. 'My daughter is very ill,' he said, 'and we're afraid she may not get better. Please come and make her well. Please come now.'

Jesus agreed to go with Jairus; but the crowd held him back. Everyone wanted to see him, to ask a question, to touch him. They were only halfway there when messengers came from the man's house and said, 'You need not bother to bring Jesus now; your little girl has died.'

Jesus comforted Jairus. 'Don't worry. Trust me.'

When they reached the house, people were wailing and crying for the little girl.

'Don't make all this noise,' said Jesus. 'The little girl is only sleeping.'

'She is not!' snorted one of the women. 'I've seen dead people, and she's dead.'

Jesus went calmly into the house, allowing just the girl's mother and father and three of his friends to come with him.

He went to where the little girl lay in bed, pale and not breathing. He took her hand. 'Little girl,' he said, 'get up.'

The girl took a breath like a loud sigh, then she sat up.

'Don't tell people about this,' said Jesus to the parents. 'Just give your daughter something to eat and take care of her.'

Jesus' friends were astonished: here was someone who was stronger than death itself.

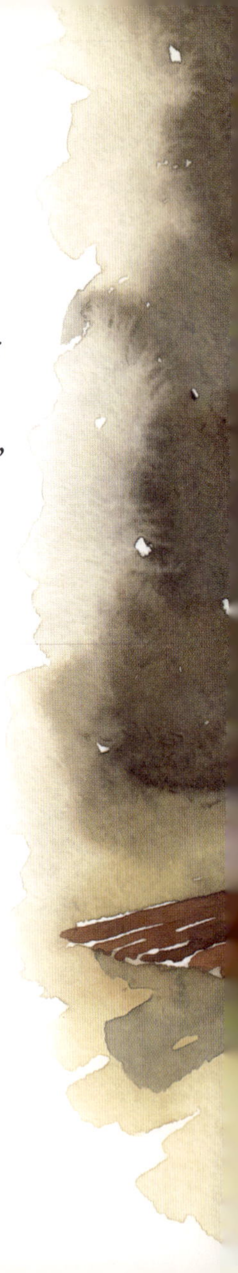

Jesus' Story of the Lost Sheep

All kinds of people wanted to hear what Jesus had to say and Jesus welcomed them all. Among the crowds there were usually quite a number of not-very-respectable people, and this made some of the others feel quite uncomfortable.

Some of the very religious people began to mutter about the situation. 'If Jesus were really from God, he wouldn't mix with those good-for-nothings,' they said.

Jesus knew what they were thinking. He told this story: 'Imagine that you were a shepherd,

with a flock of one hundred sheep. You'd know each one in its own right; you'd know exactly what made each sheep different.

'So imagine how you'd feel if one went missing.'

'You'd go looking for it straight away,' called someone in the crowd.

'Of course you'd go looking for it,' said Jesus. 'You'd leave the ninety-nine in a safe pasture and go out into the hills to search every last dip and gully.

'When you found your lost sheep, you'd pick it up carefully and carry it back home.

'Then, when you'd made the sheepfold safe for the night, you'd gather your friends together for a party,' said Jesus. 'That's how glad you'd be.'

Jesus looked directly at the religious people who had been muttering about him. 'God is like that shepherd,' he said. 'The angels in heaven celebrate when one person who has got their life in a mess changes their ways and comes back home to God.'

Jesus' Story of the Runaway Son

Jesus wanted everyone to know how much God welcomes people. He told this story: 'There was once a man who had two sons. They both worked on the family farm, and they were wealthy.

'The younger son dreamed of more exciting things. He thought of a plan and went to his father. "Half of all this will be mine when you're dead," he said unkindly. "But I want the money now."

'The father was sad. He was sure the young man was making a mistake. Still, he let him have what he wanted and waved him goodbye.

'The son went to a big city, far away. He

made sure he had a good time – always spending, throwing parties and surrounding himself with good-time friends.

'Then the harvests failed and the price of food went up everywhere. The young man ran out of money. He ran out of food. His friends were nowhere to be seen.

'Desperate and hungry, he took a job looking after pigs.

'"I've been so wrong," he sighed. "I'm even tempted to eat the pig food." Then a thought struck him. "My father's servants live better than this. I shall go home, say how sorry I am and ask to be taken on as a servant there."

'And so he set off for home. But while he was still a long way off, his father saw him coming. He ran to greet him and welcomed him with a big party.

'The older brother heard the noise. When he found out what the party was for, he was cross. "What has my selfish brother done to deserve this?" he complained. "Why don't I get a party?"

'"But everything I have is already yours," his father replied. "We must be happy today. Your brother was as good as dead, but he's come home alive. He was lost, but now he is found."'

Jesus' Story of the Good Samaritan

A man hurried through the crowd to ask Jesus a question. 'Teacher,' he said, 'what must I do to be part of God's everlasting kingdom?'

'What do the laws say?' replied Jesus.

'That I must love God completely and love my neighbour as myself.'

'That's right,' said Jesus.

'But who is my neighbour?' asked the man.

Jesus told a story: 'There was once a man who was travelling from Jerusalem to Jericho. Out in the wild hills, robbers leaped down from their cave and beat him up. They took his money and left him for dead.

'A priest came by. He saw the man and was worried. "What a dreadful thing to happen in this dreadful place," he thought.

'He hurried quickly by, staying as far away from the man as he could.

'Next came a Levite, who worked in the temple. He saw the man and walked right up to him. The man seemed dead. The Levite hurried on by.

'Then came a Samaritan,' said Jesus. Samaritans were foreigners to Jesus' listeners, and there was a lot of bad feeling between the two groups. No one would expect good things from a Samaritan.

Jesus continued his story: 'The Samaritan saw the man. He stopped and went over to him. He cleaned the man's wounds and bandaged them. Then he lifted the man onto his donkey and took him to an inn, where he took care of him.

'The next day he went to the innkeeper, money in hand. "Take care of the man for me," he said.

“If it costs more than I am giving you now, I will pay the extra when I come back this way.”

‘So the question is this,’ said Jesus. ‘Who was a neighbour to the man?’

‘The one who helped him,’ came the answer.

‘You go then and do the same,’ said Jesus.

The Man in the Tree

The people of Jericho were full of excitement. Jesus was coming to their town. The streets were already crowded, everyone jostling to get a good place.

At the back of the crowd, Zacchaeus was angry. Why had he been born short? He couldn't see a thing!

'Come on, be fair and let me get to the front,' he said bossily. The people turned to look, then turned away. They knew Zacchaeus – the man who'd made himself rich collecting their money in taxes for the Romans. Worse than that, everyone knew he charged too much. That's how tax collectors made their money. And now Zacchaeus wanted to be treated fairly? Not likely.

Zacchaeus was determined to see Jesus. Then he had an idea. He ran to a tree further along the road and climbed up. Now he had a perfect view!

At last, Jesus came along. Then he stopped,

right by the tree. He looked up. 'Come down, Zacchaeus,' he called. 'I want to come to your house.'

Zacchaeus was so surprised he nearly fell as he hurried down. He shut his ears to the muttering: 'Hmmph. Jesus is going to visit that criminal, is he? To share a meal I suppose, as if they were friends. I don't think much of that.'

Zacchaeus gave Jesus the warmest welcome. He listened as Jesus talked with him, and everything Jesus said made sense. At the end of the meal he stood up and made an announcement to everyone in the room.

‘I haven’t done good things with my life,’ he said, ‘but now I’m going to change. I’m going to give half my money to the poor, and I’m going to repay those I’ve cheated four times over.’

Jesus smiled. ‘Someone has been saved today. This is why I came: to rescue people from their bad ways and bring them home to God.’

Jesus Rides to Jerusalem

It was a day in the spring. The road to Jerusalem was crowded. People were travelling to the city from everywhere. They all wanted to celebrate the great festival of Passover at the temple.

Suddenly there was a whisper of excitement: 'Look who's coming!'

'It's Jesus! A miracle worker, so they say.'

'Some people are saying more than that! They're hoping he's going to make himself king and set our nation free.'

'Of course! He's riding to the city like a king. Let's give him a royal welcome!'

The crowds started to shout: 'Long live the king! God bless the king.'

Some cut branches from palm trees and waved them like banners. Others flung their cloaks on the ground to make a carpet for Jesus' donkey to walk on.

'Such a nice donkey,' said a little girl.

Her brother stopped cheering for a moment. 'A proper king ought to ride a war horse,' he said. 'People who are going to fight don't ride donkeys.'

'Perhaps Jesus isn't going to fight,' said the girl. 'He heals people. I don't think he wants to hurt people.'

The crowds went on cheering as Jesus went into the city. He went first to the temple. Inside the courtyards there were stalls selling the things

people needed for the festival: animals and birds to give as an offering to God, and special coins. The noise was deafening as people argued about prices. The stallholders were cheating their customers.

Jesus saw all this and he was very angry. He tipped up one of the stalls and sent the coins rolling. Then he began to drive the stallholders away.

'God says this temple is a house of prayer,' he said. 'You have made it a den of robbers.'

Some of the religious leaders were very angry. 'There's trouble ahead,' they muttered.

The Darkest Day

Jerusalem was always a lively place at Passover time. The year that Jesus rode in welcomed by a cheering crowd, it was buzzing with excitement. What was he going to do next? Was he going to free the people from their Roman enemies?

The religious leaders were very worried too. Whatever Jesus was planning, they were sure it meant trouble.

Jesus seemed only to want to go on teaching and healing; but Jesus' friend Judas wanted to make something happen. He went to a secret meeting with the religious leaders. They paid him to tip them off about where to find Jesus alone so they could arrest him.

Jesus knew that hard times lay ahead. As he shared the Passover meal with his friends, he broke the bread. 'This is my body,' he said, 'broken for you.'

Later he took the ceremonial cup of wine and shared it round. 'This is my blood,' he said. 'It is spilled for you and for many, to bring you God's forgiveness.'

Jesus' friends did not really understand what he was saying. They were glad to go together to a quiet olive grove. While Jesus prayed, they fell asleep.

Then Judas led a band of armed men to arrest Jesus. They took him to the priests, who accused him of all kinds of troublemaking. They took him to the Roman governor, Pontius Pilate, and said he was a dangerous rebel who wanted to make himself his people's king.

Pilate didn't much care. Jesus hadn't done anything to make him worried; but he wanted to keep the leaders of the people happy, so he agreed to have Jesus put to death.

Roman soldiers took Jesus outside the city and crucified him, along with two other criminals.

Jesus hung in great pain. He said a prayer aloud: 'Father, forgive them.' Soon after, he died.

The News that Changed Everything

Jesus' friends were dismayed when he was crucified. They were also frightened for themselves, and they ran away.

A wealthy admirer of Jesus named Joseph went to Pilate and asked to take the body. He had it laid in a stone tomb. As the sun set to mark the beginning of the weekly day of rest, the few who had gathered to help rolled the stone door shut.

The day of rest came and went – a day of great sadness. Early the next morning, some women went back to the tomb to prepare the body in the proper way for burial.

To their amazement, the door of the tomb had been rolled open. Two angels, dressed in white, were sitting there. 'Don't be afraid,' they said. 'Jesus is not here: he is alive. Go and tell all his friends.'

Mary Magdalene stayed behind. She stood by the tomb weeping. The angels spoke to her. 'Why are you crying?' they asked.

'Because they have taken Jesus' body,' she sobbed. She turned away. She could see a man among the olive trees. 'He must be the person who works here,' she thought. 'Maybe he can help.'

She went to ask him.

The man turned towards her. 'Mary!' he said.

At once she knew: it was Jesus.

The news that Jesus was alive spread among all his friends. They knew it was him. They saw the marks of the nails in his hands and feet. They shared meals together, as they had in the old days.

Yet they knew he was different, too, as he appeared among them even when they were together in a locked room, and disappeared just as suddenly. Jesus had passed through death on to a new kind of life, and his place was now in heaven.

'Go and tell everyone in the world about me and my message,' Jesus told his friends. 'God will give you the help you need.'

A Message for all the World

Jesus had returned to heaven. His friends had seen him go, as if wrapped in a cloud. Now they were puzzled about what to do next.

A few days later, when they were all together indoors, they heard a sound like rushing wind. They saw what looked like tongues of fire dancing over their heads. More than that, they felt brave, as never before – brave enough to tell everyone in the world the whole story of Jesus.

They hurried out into the streets of Jerusalem and began to spread the news. 'Listen to the things that Jesus taught,' they said. 'We know

that his teaching is from God. You saw him put to death on a cross, but we have seen him since then. God has raised him to new life.'

People were curious. They wanted to know more.

'This is what it all means,' said one of Jesus' friends. 'God is love. Jesus was God's son. He came to show us just how much God loves us all. He died, as we will all die. God raised him to life, and God wants to welcome us all to new life in God's kingdom as God's friends for ever.

'So let us love God; and let us love one another.'

Many people believed, and their lives were changed.

The news has been spreading ever since – news of love and joy and peace.

Introduction

Do you ever talk to God, or pray? Many people pray in church or at bedtime, but did you know that you can pray at any time and in any place? God wants us to talk to him about everything and he understands how we are feeling. Sometimes we are not sure what to say, so the prayers in this book may help. You will find prayers to say on ordinary days and on special days through the year.

If you like, you can change the words a little or add the name of the person or event you are praying for, to make a prayer just right for you to say. You will soon have some favourite prayers in this book, and others may give you ideas about what you might like to say to God.

My Very Own Prayers

Prayer is
Talking to God,
Listening to God,
Loving God.

Alison Winn

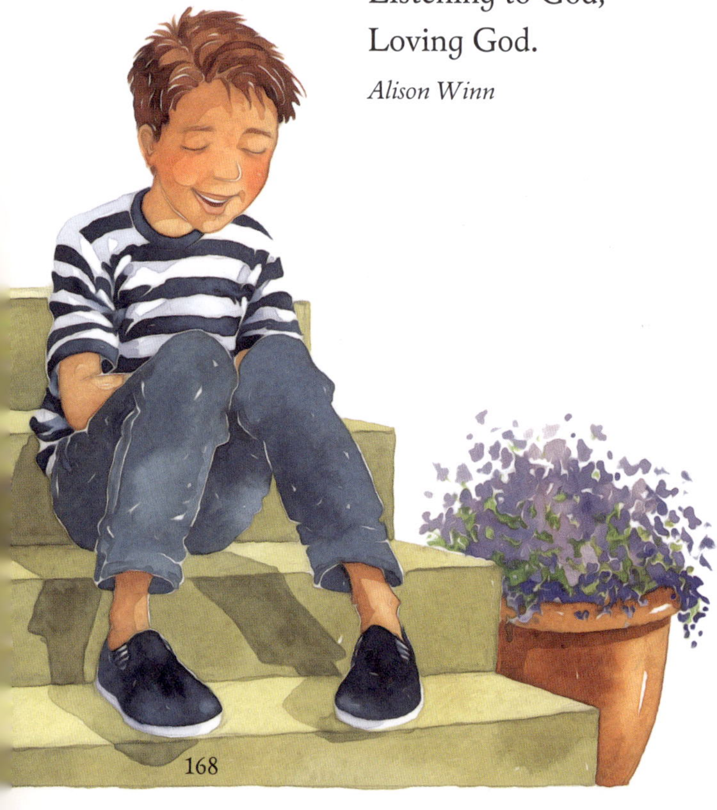

My World

Hello God

Here I am
beneath the sky
and all alone
in prayer;
but I know
God is listening,
for God is
everywhere.

Lois Rock

My head is still.
My hands are still.
My arms are still.
My feet are still.
And now I fold my hands to pray.

Author unknown

When you can't put your prayers
into words, God hears your heart.

Author unknown

Thank you, God, that you care for me
and all I do each day.
Thank you that I can pray to you
for you hear what I say.
You are there when I'm glad or sad,
and even when I'm wrong.
I praise you, God, for loving me
right now and all life long.

All About Me

Lord, you know all about me...
I praise you because you made me
In an amazing and wonderful way.

Based on Psalm 139

Thank you, God, for making me,
All that I am, and all that I can see.
Thank you too for your loving care

For all your creation everywhere.
Dear God,
Here I am: your child, full of life and eager to learn about your world.

You made me just as I am, God.
Thank you that there's no one quite like me anywhere else in the world.
That makes me feel really special.

My Family: the Grown-ups

Dear God,
Thank you for Mum and Dad who give me so much, especially lots of love. Help me to show them that I love them too.

Help me, God, to listen to my parents
and to hear the wise words they say.

Dear God,
Thank you for my mum and dad;
They've lots to do today.
Help them finish really soon
So we'll have time to play.

Dear God, it can't be easy to grow old. Give me patience when Granny and Grandad forget things. Help me to listen when they want to talk. One day I'll be old too.

My Family: Brothers and Sisters

Dear God,
It's not always easy to have brothers or sisters. But sometimes it's really great. Please help us to get along together.

Dear God,
Sometimes I wish I had a brother or sister to play with. Please help me not to feel lonely.

We're so happy to have a new baby in our family. Thank you, God!

Dear God, thank you for my sister.
She always understands how I feel.
Olwen Turchetta

My Family: All Together

God bless all those that I love;
God bless all those that love me;
God bless all those that love those that I love
And all those that love those that love me.

From a New England sampler

Thank you for the love we show
when we hug each other.

Dear God,
I'm glad that your son, Jesus, lived in a family. He knows the fun and the difficult things about living with others. Help our family to be happy, safe and loving.

Our Home

Mum says that our home is more than a house because it is furnished with love. Thank you, God, for my family and for your love.

Dear God, I pray for children
who live in unhappy homes.
Please help them not to be sad.

May our home be happy
May our home be safe
May our home be loving
May our home be blessed.

Lois Rock

Bless this house which is our home
May we welcome all who come.

Anonymous

Bless all animals both big and small
That fly and swim and leap.
Protect and care for them all –
The wild ones and the pets we keep.

Deborah Lock

My Day

In the Morning

This morning, God,
This is your day.
I am your child,
Show me your way.
Amen

Author unknown

This is the day the Lord has made;
let us rejoice and be glad in it.

Psalm 118:24

Father, we thank you for the night,
And for the pleasant morning light;
For rest and food and loving care,
And all that makes the day so fair.
Help us to do the things we should,
To be to others kind and good;
In all we do at work or play
To grow more loving every day.

Author unknown

Dear God,
Thank you for this new day.
Amen

At Mealtimes

God is great, God is good,
Let us thank him for our food.

Traditional

Each time we eat,
May we remember God's love.

A Chinese grace

For what we are about to receive
May the Lord make us truly thankful.

Traditional

May this food give us strength
To be good and kind in all we do.

Deborah Lock

The bread is warm and fresh,
The water cool and clear.
Lord of all life, be with us,
Lord of all life, be near.

An African grace

For good food and good friends to share it,
thank you, God.

At School

Lord Jesus Christ, be with me today,
And help me in all I think, or do, or say.

Traditional

Bless to me, O Lord,
the work of my hands.
Bless to me, O God,
the work of my mind.
Bless to me, O God,
the work of my heart.

Author unknown

Dear God,
When I don't know the right answer,
please help me ask the right question.

Lois Rock

Dear God, every day I learn something new.
Thank you that the world is
so full of amazing things.

Sarah Medina

At Play

Thank you, God, for time to play,
To skip and jump and run,
With friends or on my own,
Laughing and having fun.

Deborah Lock

Computer games and model trains and skates and bikes and kites. We thank you, God, for all the different ways we can enjoy playing together.

Dear God, help me to be a good loser.

Help me to share and be kind
When I play with others.
Let me show love and patience
When I am with them.

Deborah Lock

Dear God,
Thank you for sunny days when I can play outside with my friends and for rainy days when I can enjoy reading my books.

Olwen Turchetta

My Friends

Thank you for the happy times
I shared with my friends today.
Thank you for the memories
We'll enjoy another day.

Dear God,
Thank you for my friend next door,
And my friend across the street,
And please help me to be a friend
To each and every one I meet.
Amen

Anonymous

Thank you, God, that none of us is quite the same. I like having friends who enjoy playing and sharing different things with me.

Thank you, God, for all my friends. Help me to be a good friend and not to argue or let them down. Thank you, most of all, for being my best friend.

For lonely children everywhere
Who do not have someone to care.
Dear God, I pray that you will send
A loving, kind and special friend.

Author unknown

Dear God,
Help me not to tread thoughtlessly
on the feelings of my friends.

Dear God,
Forgive me for saying hurtful things to my friend.
Give me the courage to say that I'm sorry, and
help me to be gentle with my words.

Dear God,
Help me to be friendly to those who have
no friends.

Dear God,
When others are sad, help me to comfort them,
just as my friends comfort me.

At Night

Dear God, sometimes I get scared in the dark. Help me to remember that you are right here with me, so I am never really alone.

Now I lay me down to sleep,
I pray thee, Lord, thy child to keep;
Thy love to guard me through the night
And wake me in the morning light.

Traditional

Now the day is over,
Night is drawing nigh,
Shadows of the evening
Steal across the sky.

Through the long night-watches
May thine angels spread
Their white wings above me,
Watching round my bed.

Sabine Baring-Gould

Lord, keep us safe this night,
Secure from all our fears;
May angels guard us while we sleep,
Till morning light appears.

John Leland

Day is done,
Gone the sun
From the lake,
From the hills,
From the sky.
Safely rest,
All is well!
God is nigh.

Anonymous

When I lie down, I go to sleep in peace;
you alone, O Lord, keep me perfectly safe.

Psalm 4:8

Our World

The World Around Us

All things bright and beautiful,
All creatures great and small,
All things wise and wonderful,
The Lord God made them all.

Mrs C.F. Alexander

Lord God Almighty,
how great and wonderful
are your deeds!

Revelation 15:3

Dear God,
Thank you for making this
wonderful world. There's so
much to see and so many
things to enjoy.

God made the world so broad and grand
Filled with blessing from his hand.
He made the sky so high and blue,
And all the little children, too.

Anonymous

Creator God, we praise you for our world: for the high snowy mountains and fertile green valleys, the leafy jungles and sandy deserts, and rivers that flow into the sea. Thank you for making so many wonderful, different places.

Dear God,
May we learn to see the world as you see it.
May we learn to care for the world as you do.

O God, the more I explore your world,
the more I marvel at it.

God, who made the earth,
The air, the sky, the sea,
Who gave the light its birth,
Careth for me.

God, who made the grass,
The flower, the fruit, the tree,
The day and night to pass,
Careth for me.

God, who made all things,
On earth, in air, in sea,
Who changing seasons brings,
Careth for me.

Sarah Betts Rhodes

People of the World

From all that dwells below the skies,
Let faith and hope with joy arise;
Let beauty, truth and good be sung
Through every land, by every tongue.

A Unitarian prayer

This I know in heaven above,
All hope and joy are there.
In the circle of God's love,
There's room for all –
And to spare.

A spiritual

Dear Lord, Creator of the world,
Help us to love one another,
Help us care for one another
As sister or as brother.
May friendship grow
From nation to nation.
Bring peace to our world
Dear Lord of Creation.

Anonymous

All God's Creatures

O God, help me to be kind
to all living things.

Dear God,
Thank you for making so many different animals. Help us to learn to treat them well so that we may all enjoy sharing your world.

Dear God,
Help me to remember that even scary animals and insects and snakes are part of your creation and should be treated with respect.

He prayeth best, who loveth best
All things both great and small;
For the dear God who loveth us,
He made and loveth all.

Samuel Taylor Coleridge

Bless the wild animals of the forest,
The mountains and the valleys,
On the plains and in the oceans.
Thank you for all your amazing creatures
That live upon this earth.

Deborah Lock

Dear Lord, care for and bless your little creatures:
The singing birds and buzzing bees,
The busy bugs and slithering snails
That shelter underground and in the trees.

Deborah Lock

Praise God for the animals
for the colours of them,
for the spots and stripes of them,
for the patches and plains of them,
their claws and paws.

Lynn Warren

Animals great, animals small,
Thank you, God, that you care for them all.

In Town

Bless all people who live and work
In towns and cities around the world.
Protect their streets
And keep their homes safe.

Deborah Lock

Busy shops and crowded places,
Hectic day and night.
Noisy streets and unknown faces,
Bustle, sounds and light.
All exciting, sometimes frightening,
Town life can be hard,
But you're with us, caring for us
Thank you, Father God.

Please make this town safe
for young and old,
for rich and poor,
and for people of all races
and places.

In the Country

Dear God,
Thank you for making the beautiful countryside. Help us not to spoil it for other people or for the animals that live there.

Thank you for wide, open places, where we can run and play in the fresh air and listen to the sounds of the country.

For flowers that bloom about our feet,
Father, we thank Thee,
For tender grass so fresh and sweet,
Father, we thank Thee,
For the song of bird and hum of bee,
For all things fair we hear or see,
Father in heaven, we thank Thee.

Ralph Waldo Emerson

I thank you, God,
for the high skies
that stretch up
to heaven.

The Weather

Dear Lord on high
Make a clear sky
Make the day fine
And let the sweet sun shine.

Traditional

Dear God, thank you for the rain which cleans our world and gives us water.

The sun may shine
The snow may fall
God will always
Love us all.

Victoria Tebbs

If I had my way I'd pray
to have fine weather every day.
But farmers need refreshing rain
and then warm sun to ripen grain.
So, dear God, I pray tonight
you'll send the weather you think right.

The Seasons

Thank you, Creator God, for the unchanging pattern of the seasons that tells of your never-ending love for your world.

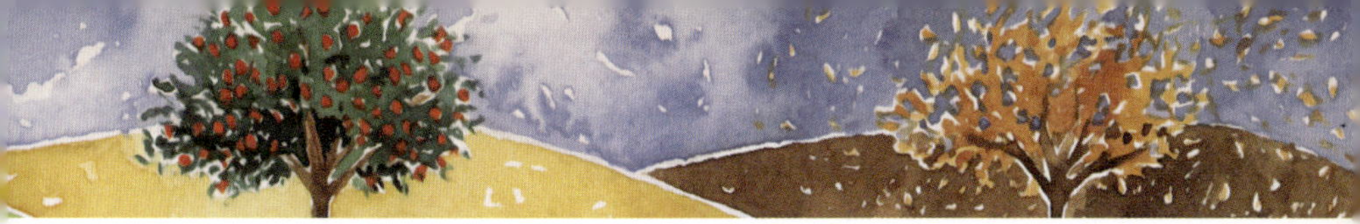

Thank you, God, that we can use
our senses to enjoy:
... seeing the bright spring colours
... smelling the scent of summer flowers
... tasting the juicy autumn fruits
... touching the soft winter snow
and hearing birdsong all year long.

Thank you for the cycle of the seasons:
The new life and spring rains,
The warm sunshine and the fruitful harvest,
And then a time of rest.

Deborah Lock

Caring for the World

Dear God,
I'm sorry we have spoiled your world. Please help us to look after it better. Help us to care for the land and all that grows on it and to save all the animals in danger.

Generous God,
I know you give me all I need –
To ask for more is sometimes greed.
But many people are quite poor;
I ask that you will give them more.
Amen

People don't always care.
They make wild creatures rare,
cutting down all the trees,
polluting lakes and seas.
We're sorry for this mess –
it must cause you distress.
We need to change things now,
so please, God, show us how.

Dear God,
You planted the Garden of Eden.
May we treat the wild lands as sacred.
You built the Heavenly City.
May we know that we build our cities
on holy ground.

Lois Rock

Sad Days

Illness

Dear God, when I am in pain please comfort me.

Thank you, God, for doctors, nurses and the many other people who help sick people to get better. Please bless their work of healing.

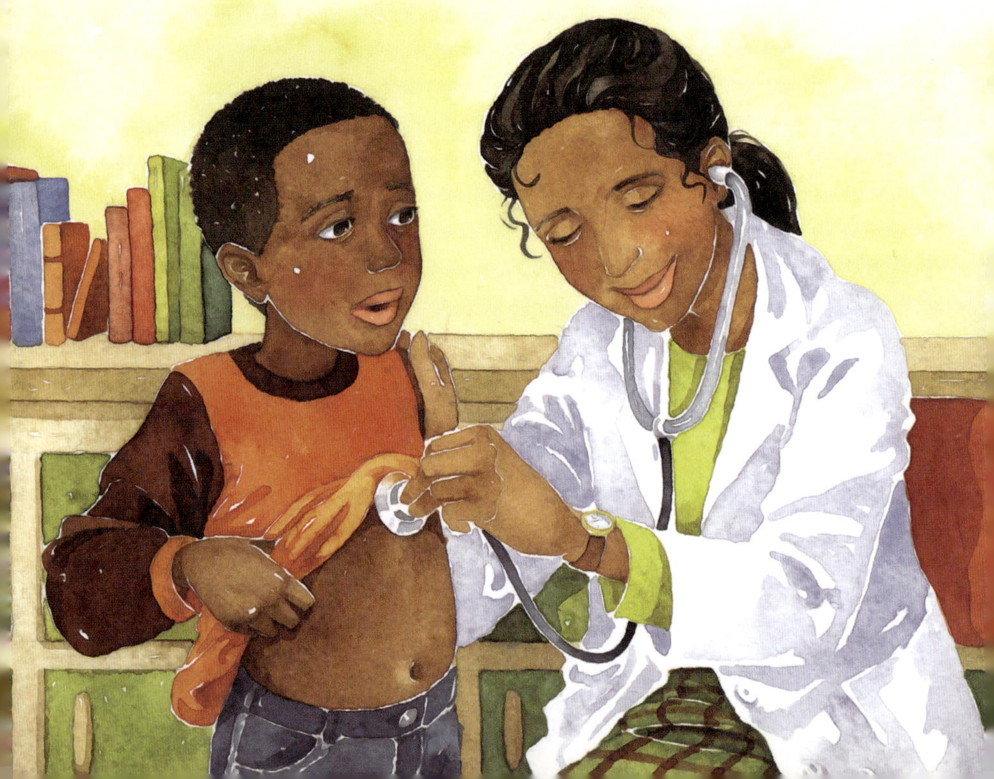

Dear God,
I feel poorly today. Please help me to get well soon and to be patient until I feel better.

Loving God,
Be close to those who are ill;
Comfort those who are worried;
Help those who are in pain.
May they know your love and care.

Help me, kind God, to show your love and kindness to my friends and family when they are ill.

The Hardest Goodbye

Every day
in silence we remember
those whom we loved
to whom we have said a last goodbye.
Every day
in silence we remember.

Lois Rock

Dear God,
You know how it
feels when someone
you love dies. Please
be close to me now as
I feel so sad.
Amen

I didn't like saying
my last goodbye
today, God. Then
I remembered that
those you love have
a new home in
heaven.

Difficult Days

Dear God,
I have a difficult decision to make today.
Help me to do the right thing.

Dear God,
It's hard when people don't understand me.
Thank you that you know me better than anyone else.

Jesus, you know what it is like to stand up for what is right. Sometimes you had to face people who were unfriendly and unkind. Help me when I have to do the same.

Dear God,
Help me to see my faults more clearly
than the wrongdoings of other people.

Dear God,
Knowing you are with me when I'm sad is like knowing that the sun is only hidden behind the clouds.

Sometimes we're mean and selfish, God,
And spoil somebody's day.
You are loving and fair to all;
Help us to live your way.

Someone hurt my feelings today.
Now I feel bad about them and
it won't be easy to forgive them.
Please help me to treat that person
the way I want to be treated.

Dear God,
I am sorry for what I've done wrong
and I ask that you will forgive me.

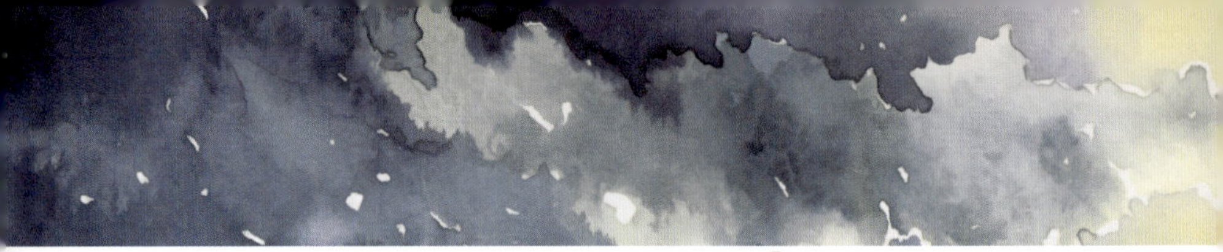

When Things Go Wrong

Dear God,
Bring peace to the whole world.

There are many bad things happening in the world. People are fighting, some have nowhere to live and many don't have enough food to eat. Please show us how we can help, God.

Lord, I know you love what is fair and hate it when people put others down and do all kinds of wrong things. Please help more people to think as you do.

Based on Amos 2:6–7

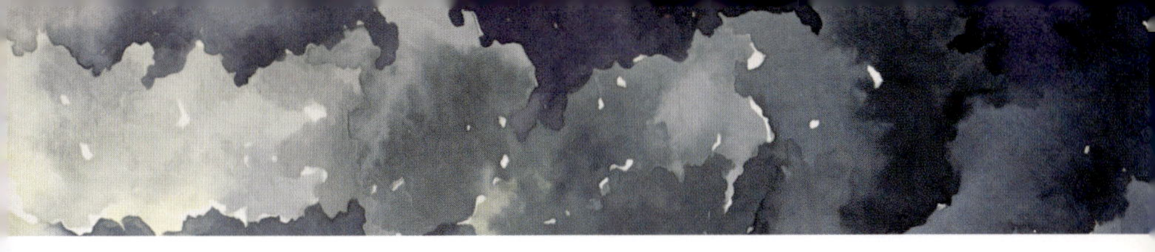

Dear God, please help people who are being treated unfairly or facing danger not to be afraid.

Amen

Please Help, God

Lord God,
Help me to become the person
you want me to be.

Please bring:
Peace in my heart;
Peace in my home;
Peace in my street;
Peace in my world.

Lois Rock

Father God, help me to enjoy the things I have and not to always want more.

O God, I don't understand why bad things happen to good people; but I want to learn to do good things even to bad people.

Lois Rock

Dear God, when I'm scared please help me to remember that you are stronger than anything that frightens me.

Happy Days

Holidays

Thank you, God,
For special days to look forward to,
and special days to remember.

Felicity Henderson

For days at home and far away
I thank you God today.
For friends and family come to stay
I thank you God today.
For Mum and Dad and time to play
I thank you God today.
For all the fun of our holiday
I thank you God today.

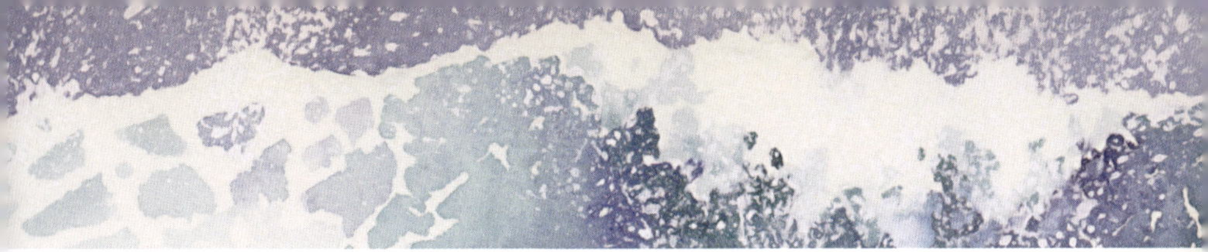

Thank you, God, for this summer day,
Thank you, God, for this golden day,
Thank you, God, for this lazy day,
Thank you, God, for our holiday.

Lois Rock

Birthdays

Guide me in my growing older,
Wiser, gentler,
Braver, bolder.

Lois Rock

Dear God,
Thank you for my birthday
And all I've done this year.
Some things were good,
Some times were sad,
But you were always near.

Thank you, God, for my birthday. The party was fun, the presents were great and everyone made me feel really special. Help me to remember to give and share, so that I can make other people's birthdays special too.

Father God, please be with me in all that happens in this new year.

Sundays

Thank you, God, for all you have done for us.
Let people everywhere praise you!

Based on Psalm 67:7

Thank you, kind God, for your day of rest.
May we spend its hours on things that bring
us joy.

Lois Rock

After you had made the world
You had a day of rest
When we get too busy, Lord,
Remind us your plan's best.

May I feel you very near
When I stop to pray.
Help me listen when you send
A message for today.

At Christmas

Thank you, God, for all the presents we receive at Christmas. Help me to remember that all happiness comes from you.

Dear God, please give your love to anyone who has no one to love them at Christmas.

Thank you, God, for showing your love by giving us the best present ever – your son, Jesus. Help us to share Christmas love with everyone we meet.

Thank you for sending Jesus to be the light of the world and to show your light.

At Easter

Thank you, God, for loving us so much.
Thank you Jesus for suffering for us.
Thank you for freeing us to be with you.
Help us to love you so much, too.

Deborah Lock

Dear Lord, you knew pain and loneliness,
But you turn sadness into joy,
And death into life.

A child's prayer

On Good Friday you died on a cross
Then laid in a tomb with a stone door.
On Easter Sunday you rose again
And were alive with us for evermore.
All thanks and praise to God.

Deborah Lock

Friday sunset, black and red.
Weep, for Jesus Christ is dead.
Sunday sunrise, white and gold.
Christ is risen, as foretold.

Lois Rock

Jesus Christ is risen today.
Alleluia!

Based on Surrexit Christus hodie

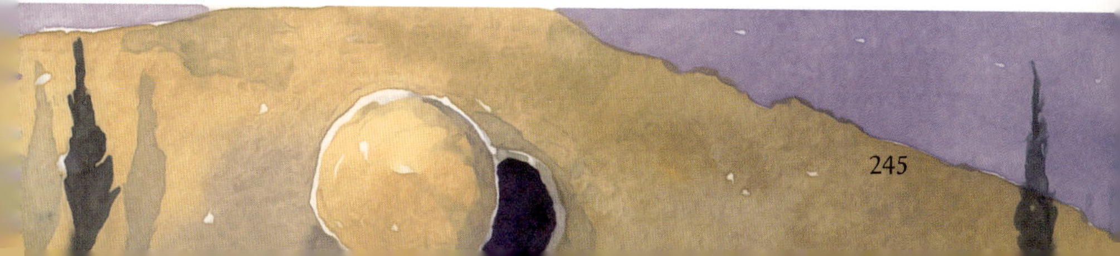

Harvest

Dear God in paradise
Look upon our sowing:
Bless the little gardens
And the green things growing.

Anonymous

O God, you show your care for the land by sending rain; you make it rich and fertile. What a rich harvest your goodness provides!

Psalm 65:9, 11

Thank you, God, for giving us a good harvest. All that you give us you mean us to share. Help us to share these gifts with others so that the world may be a better place.

The sun and the rain,
The seeds that bring grain,
The fruit and the flowers,
That grow with the showers.
Thank you, God, for all
your harvest gifts.

Thank You, God

Dear God, thank you that each one of us is special to you and that you love and care for us always.

Sing to God with thankfulness,
Sing a song of praise,
Sing out loud and joyfully,
Sing out all your days.

From Psalm 95

Thank you, Lord, for dying for us. Thank you for loving us even though we do things wrong and sometimes forget you.

Lord, it is good to give you thanks
from morning to night.

Based on Psalm 92:1–2

Glory to God for everything!

St John Chrysostom

You're Great, God!

Sing praise to the Lord!
Sing praise!

Based on Psalm 47:6

I praise you, God, for your great love for each one of us. Help me to light up my world with your love.

> O God, your greatness is seen in all the world,
> In everything and everyone,
> Everywhere and in every way.
>
> *Deborah Lock*

Please fill my life, O Lord my God,
In every part with praise,
That every day I'll show to all
Your being and your ways.

After Horatius Bonar

Our Father God,
We want you to be our King for ever:
then everyone will live as you want.
Give us each day all that we need.
Forgive us for the wrong things we do,
as we forgive people who hurt us.
Help us stop wanting to do bad things.
And keep us from all harm.
Amen

Adapted from the prayer Jesus taught,
the Lord's Prayer

First Line Index

Acknowledgments

All unattributed prayers are by Su Box, copyright © 2003 Lion Hudson IP Limited. Prayers by Alison Winn (p. 168), Felicity Henderson (p. 236), Deborah Lock (pp. 182, 187, 190, 191, 208, 210, 217, 244, 245 & 250), Sarah Medina (p. 189), Lois Rock (pp. 170, 180, 189, 220, 224, 232, 237, 238, 241 & 245), Victoria Tebbs (p. 215) and Olwen Turchetta (pp. 176 & 191) are copyright © Lion Hudson IP Limited. Scripture quotation (p. 185) taken from the Holy Bible, New International Version, copyright © 1973, 1978, 1984 by International Bible Society. Used by permission of Hodder & Stoughton Limited. All rights reserved. 'NIV' is a registered trademark of International Bible Society. UK trademark number 1448790. Scriptures (pp. 198, 200, 247) quoted from the Good News Bible published by The Bible Societies/HarperCollins Publishers Ltd, UK © American Bible Society 1966, 1971, 1976, 1992, used with permission.